A Treasury of Psalms
© Frances Lincoln Limited 2000

First published in Great Britain in 2000 by
Frances Lincoln Limited,
4 Torriano Mews,
Torriano Avenue, London NW5 2RZ

Published in the United States of America by the J. Paul Getty Museum,
1200 Getty Center Drive, Los Angeles, California 90049–1687

For photographic acknowledgments and copyright details, see page 77

Psalms and images selected by Yvonne Whiteman

Set in Bembo
Printed in Hong Kong
1 3 5 7 9 8 6 4 2

A Treasury of Psalms

THE J. PAUL GETTY MUSEUM, LOS ANGELES

I will sing a new song unto thee, O God:
upon a psaltery and an instrument of ten strings
will I sing praises unto thee.

from PSALM 144

Janet L. Avery
Christmas 2000
from Sao & John

CONTENTS

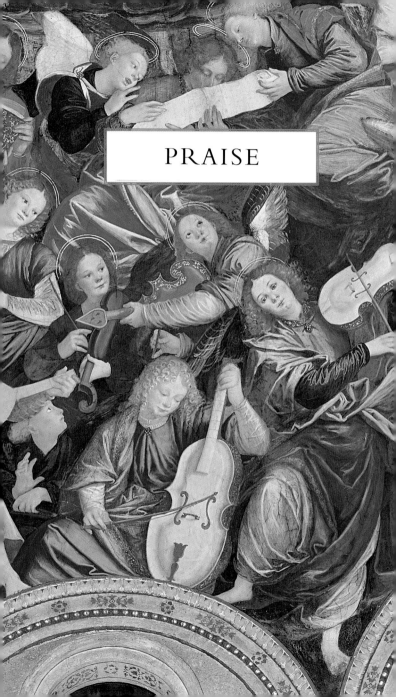

PRAISE

OCLAP YOUR HANDS, all ye people;
shout unto God with the voice of
triumph.

For the Lord most high is terrible;
  he is a great King over all the earth.
He shall subdue the people under us,
  and the nations under our feet.
He shall choose our inheritance for us,
  the excellency of Jacob whom he loved.
God is gone up with a shout, the Lord
  with the sound of a trumpet.
Sing praises to God, sing praises:
  sing praises unto our King, sing praises.
For God is the King of all the earth:
  sing ye praises with understanding.
God reigneth over the heathen:
  God sitteth upon the throne of his holiness.
The princes of the people are gathered together,
  even the people of the God of Abraham:
  for the shields of the earth belong unto God:
  he is greatly exalted.

PSALM 47

GOD BE MERCIFUL unto us, and bless us;
and cause his face to shine upon us;
That thy way may be known upon earth,
thy saving health among all nations.
Let the people praise thee, O God;
let all the people praise thee.
O let the nations be glad and sing for joy:
for thou shalt judge the people righteously,

and govern the nations upon earth.
Let the people praise thee, O God;
   let all the people praise thee.
Then shall the earth yield her increase;
   and God, even our own God, shall bless us.
God shall bless us; and all the ends of the
   earth shall fear him.

PSALM 67

O SING UNTO THE LORD a new song:
sing unto the Lord, all the earth.
Sing unto the Lord, bless his name;
shew forth his salvation from day to day.
Declare his glory among the heathen,
his wonders among all people.
For the Lord is great, and greatly to be praised:
he is to be feared above all gods.
For all the gods of the nations are idols:
but the Lord made the heavens.
Honour and majesty are before him:
strength and beauty are in his sanctuary.
Give unto the Lord, O ye kindreds of the people,
give unto the Lord glory and strength.
Give unto the Lord the glory due unto his name:
bring an offering, and come into his courts.
O worship the Lord in the beauty of
holiness: fear before him, all the earth.

from PSALM 96

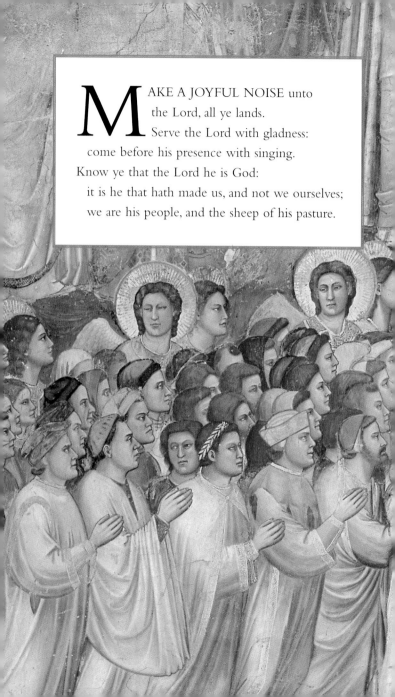

MAKE A JOYFUL NOISE unto the Lord, all ye lands.
Serve the Lord with gladness:
come before his presence with singing.
Know ye that the Lord he is God:
it is he that hath made us, and not we ourselves;
we are his people, and the sheep of his pasture.

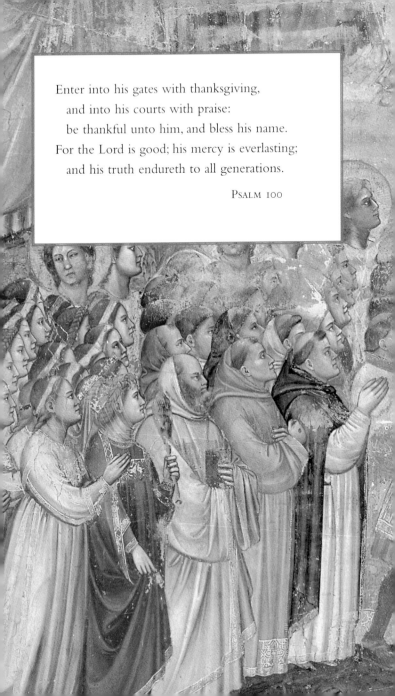

Enter into his gates with thanksgiving,
  and into his courts with praise:
  be thankful unto him, and bless his name.
For the Lord is good; his mercy is everlasting;
  and his truth endureth to all generations.

PSALM 100

O GIVE THANKS unto the
Lord; for he is good:
for his mercy endureth for ever.
O give thanks unto the God of gods:
   for his mercy endureth for ever.
O give thanks to the Lord of Lords:
   for his mercy endureth for ever.
To him who alone doeth great wonders:
   for his mercy endureth for ever.
To him that by wisdom made the heavens:
   for his mercy endureth for ever.
To him that stretched out the earth
   above the waters:
   for his mercy endureth for ever.

from PSALM 136

PRAISE YE THE LORD.
Praise God in his sanctuary: praise
him in the firmament of his power.
Praise him for his mighty acts:
   praise him according to his excellent greatness.
Praise him with the sound of the trumpet:
   praise him with the psaltery and harp.
Praise him with the timbrel and dance:
   praise him with stringed instruments and organs.
Praise him upon the loud cymbals:
   praise him upon the high sounding cymbals.
Let every thing that hath breath praise the Lord.
   Praise ye the Lord.

PSALM 150

CELEBRATION

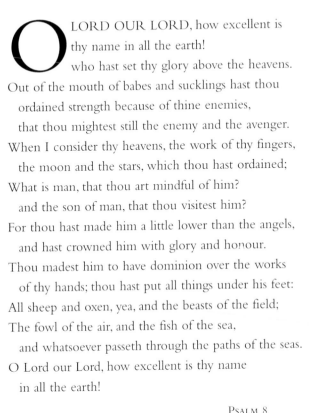

O LORD OUR LORD, how excellent is
thy name in all the earth!
who hast set thy glory above the heavens.
Out of the mouth of babes and sucklings hast thou
ordained strength because of thine enemies,
that thou mightest still the enemy and the avenger.
When I consider thy heavens, the work of thy fingers,
the moon and the stars, which thou hast ordained;
What is man, that thou art mindful of him?
and the son of man, that thou visitest him?
For thou hast made him a little lower than the angels,
and hast crowned him with glory and honour.
Thou madest him to have dominion over the works
of thy hands; thou hast put all things under his feet:
All sheep and oxen, yea, and the beasts of the field;
The fowl of the air, and the fish of the sea,
and whatsoever passeth through the paths of the seas.
O Lord our Lord, how excellent is thy name
in all the earth!

PSALM 8

THE HEAVENS declare the glory of God; and the firmament sheweth his handywork. Day unto day uttereth speech, and night unto night sheweth knowledge.

There is no speech nor language, where their voice is not heard.

Their line is gone out through all the earth, and their words to the end of the world. In them hath he set a tabernacle for the sun,

Which is as a bridegroom coming out of his chamber, and rejoiceth as a strong man to run a race.

His going forth is from the end of the heaven, and his circuit unto the ends of it: and there is nothing hid from the heat thereof.

The law of the Lord is perfect, converting the soul: the testimony of the Lord is sure, making wise the simple.

The statutes of the Lord are right, rejoicing the heart: the commandment of the Lord is pure, enlightening the eyes.

The fear of the Lord is clean, enduring for ever: the judgments of the Lord are true and righteous altogether.

More to be desired are they than gold, yea, than much fine gold: sweeter also than honey and the honeycomb.

from PSALM 19

THE EARTH is the Lord's, and the fulness thereof; the world, and they that dwell therein.

For he hath founded it upon the seas, and established it upon the floods.

Who shall ascend into the hill of the Lord? or who shall stand in his holy place?

He that hath clean hands, and a pure heart; who hath not lifted up his soul unto vanity, nor sworn deceitfully.

He shall receive the blessing from the Lord, and righteousness from the God of his salvation.

This is the generation of them that seek him, that seek thy face, O Jacob.

Lift up your heads, O ye gates; and be ye lift up, ye everlasting doors; and the King of glory shall come in.

Who is this King of glory? The Lord strong and mighty, the Lord mighty in battle.

Lift up your heads, O ye gates; even lift them up, ye everlasting doors; and the King of glory shall come in.

Who is this King of glory? The Lord of hosts, he is the King of glory.

PSALM 24

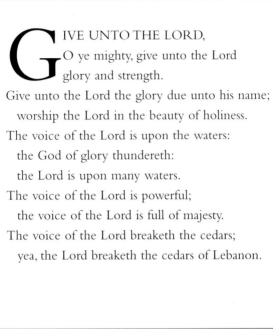

GIVE UNTO THE LORD,
O ye mighty, give unto the Lord
glory and strength.
Give unto the Lord the glory due unto his name;
    worship the Lord in the beauty of holiness.
The voice of the Lord is upon the waters:
    the God of glory thundereth:
    the Lord is upon many waters.
The voice of the Lord is powerful;
    the voice of the Lord is full of majesty.
The voice of the Lord breaketh the cedars;
    yea, the Lord breaketh the cedars of Lebanon.

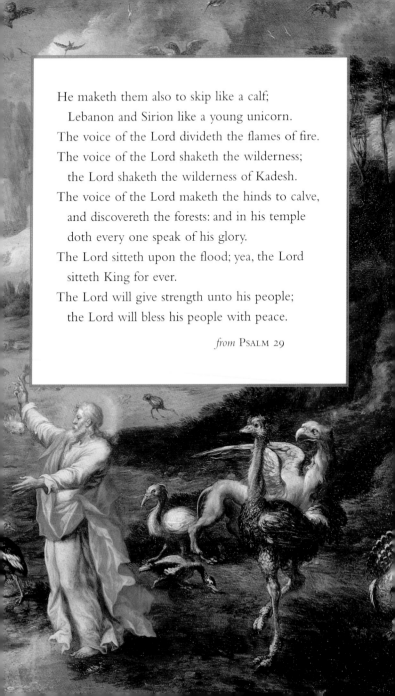

He maketh them also to skip like a calf;
   Lebanon and Sirion like a young unicorn.
The voice of the Lord divideth the flames of fire.
The voice of the Lord shaketh the wilderness;
   the Lord shaketh the wilderness of Kadesh.
The voice of the Lord maketh the hinds to calve,
   and discovereth the forests: and in his temple
   doth every one speak of his glory.
The Lord sitteth upon the flood; yea, the Lord
   sitteth King for ever.
The Lord will give strength unto his people;
   the Lord will bless his people with peace.

from PSALM 29

GOD IS OUR REFUGE and strength,
a very present help in trouble.
Therefore will not we fear, though
the earth be removed, and though the mountains
be carried into the midst of the sea;
Though the waters thereof roar and be troubled,
though the mountains shake with the swelling
thereof.
There is a river, the streams whereof shall
make glad the city of God, the holy place
of the tabernacles of the most High.
God is in the midst of her; she shall not be moved:
God shall help her, and that right early.
The heathen raged, the kingdoms were moved:
he uttered his voice, the earth melted.
The Lord of hosts is with us; the God of Jacob
is our refuge.

from PSALM 46

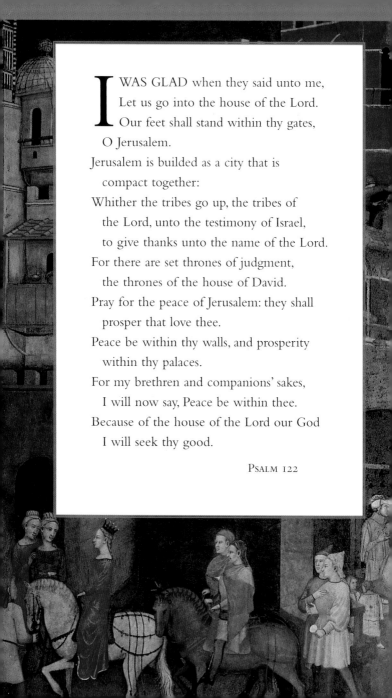

I WAS GLAD when they said unto me,
Let us go into the house of the Lord.
Our feet shall stand within thy gates,
O Jerusalem.
Jerusalem is builded as a city that is
compact together:
Whither the tribes go up, the tribes of
the Lord, unto the testimony of Israel,
to give thanks unto the name of the Lord.
For there are set thrones of judgment,
the thrones of the house of David.
Pray for the peace of Jerusalem: they shall
prosper that love thee.
Peace be within thy walls, and prosperity
within thy palaces.
For my brethren and companions' sakes,
I will now say, Peace be within thee.
Because of the house of the Lord our God
I will seek thy good.

PSALM 122

BLESSED IS EVERY ONE that feareth the Lord; that walketh in his ways.

For thou shalt eat the labour of thine hands: happy shalt thou be, and it shall be well with thee.

Thy wife shall be as a fruitful vine by the sides of thine house: thy children like olive plants round about thy table.

Behold, that thus shall the man be blessed that feareth the Lord.

The Lord shall bless thee out of Zion: and thou shalt see the good of Jerusalem all the days of thy life.

Yea, thou shalt see thy children's children, and peace upon Israel.

PSALM 128

BEHOLD, HOW GOOD and how pleasant it is for brethren to dwell together in unity! It is like the precious ointment upon the head, that ran down upon the beard, even Aaron's beard: that went down to the skirts of his garments;

As the dew of Hermon, and as the dew that
descended upon the mountains of Zion: for
there the Lord commanded the blessing, even
life for evermore.

PSALM 133

BLESSED BE THE LORD my strength,
which teacheth my hands to war,
and my fingers to fight:
My goodness, and my fortress; my high tower,
and my deliverer; my shield, and he in whom I trust;
who subdueth my people under me.
Lord, what is man, that thou takest knowledge of him!
or the son of man, that thou makest account of him!
Man is like to vanity: his days are as a shadow
that passeth away.
Bow thy heavens, O Lord, and come down:
touch the mountains, and they shall smoke.
Cast forth lightning, and scatter them: shoot out
thine arrows, and destroy them.
Send thine hand from above; rid me, and deliver me
out of great waters, from the hand of strange children;
Whose mouth speaketh vanity, and their right hand
is a right hand of falsehood.
I will sing a new song unto thee, O God:
upon a psaltery and an instrument of ten strings
will I sing praises unto thee.

from PSALM 144

SUPPLICATION

HAVE MERCY upon me, O God,
according to thy loving kindness:
according unto the multitude of thy
tender mercies blot out my transgressions.

Wash me throughly from mine iniquity, and cleanse
me from my sin.

For I acknowledge my transgressions: and my sin
is ever before me.

Against thee, thee only, have I sinned, and done
this evil in thy sight: that thou mightest be justified
when thou speakest, and be clear when thou judgest.

Behold, I was shapen in iniquity; and in sin did my
mother conceive me.

Behold, thou desirest truth in the inward parts:
and in the hidden part thou shalt make me to
know wisdom.

Purge me with hyssop, and I shall be clean:
wash me, and I shall be whiter than snow.

Make me to hear joy and gladness; that the bones
which thou hast broken may rejoice.

Hide thy face from my sins, and blot out
all mine iniquities.

Create in me a clean heart, O God;
and renew a right spirit within me.

from PSALM 51

HOW AMIABLE are thy tabernacles,
     O Lord of hosts!
          My soul longeth, yea, even fainteth
     for the courts of the Lord: my heart and my flesh
     crieth out for the living God.
Yea, the sparrow hath found an house, and
     the swallow a nest for herself, where she may lay
     her young, even thine altars, O Lord of hosts,
     my King, and my God.
Blessed are they that dwell in thy house:
     they will be still praising thee.
Blessed is the man whose strength is in thee;
     in whose heart are the ways of them.
Who passing through the valley of Baca
     make it a well; the rain also filleth the pools.
They go from strength to strength, every one
     of them in Zion appeareth before God.
O Lord God of hosts, hear my prayer: give ear,
     O God of Jacob.

from PSALM 84

HEAR MY PRAYER, O Lord,
and let my cry come unto thee.
Hide not thy face from me in the day
when I am in trouble; incline thine ear unto me:
in the day when I call answer me speedily.
For my days are consumed like smoke,
and my bones are burned as an hearth.
My heart is smitten, and withered like grass;
so that I forget to eat my bread.
By reason of the voice of my groaning
my bones cleave to my skin.
I am like a pelican of the wilderness:
I am like an owl of the desert.
I watch, and am as a sparrow alone upon
the house top.
Mine enemies reproach me all the day; and they
that are mad against me are sworn against me.
For I have eaten ashes like bread, and mingled
my drink with weeping.
Because of thine indignation and thy wrath:
for thou hast lifted me up, and cast me down.
My days are like a shadow that declineth;
and I am withered like grass.
But thou, O Lord, shall endure for ever;
and thy remembrance unto all generations.

from PSALM 102

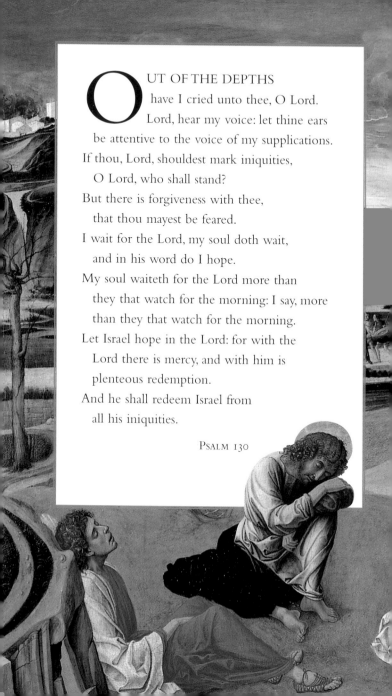

OUT OF THE DEPTHS
have I cried unto thee, O Lord.
Lord, hear my voice: let thine ears
be attentive to the voice of my supplications.
If thou, Lord, shouldest mark iniquities,
   O Lord, who shall stand?
But there is forgiveness with thee,
   that thou mayest be feared.
I wait for the Lord, my soul doth wait,
   and in his word do I hope.
My soul waiteth for the Lord more than
   they that watch for the morning: I say, more
   than they that watch for the morning.
Let Israel hope in the Lord: for with the
   Lord there is mercy, and with him is
   plenteous redemption.
And he shall redeem Israel from
   all his iniquities.

PSALM 130

L ORD, MY HEART is not haughty,
nor mine eyes lofty: neither do I
exercise myself in great matters,
or in things too high for me.

Surely I have behaved and quieted myself,
as a child that is weaned of his mother:
my soul is even as a weaned child.

Let Israel hope in the Lord from henceforth
and for ever.

PSALM 131

MEDITATION

LORD, WHO SHALL abide in thy tabernacle?
who shall dwell in thy holy hill?
He that walketh uprightly, and worketh
righteousness, and speaketh the truth in his heart.
He that backbiteth not with his tongue,
nor doeth evil to his neighbour, nor taketh up
a reproach against his neighbour.
In whose eyes a vile person is contemned;
but he honoureth them that fear the Lord.
He that sweareth to his own hurt, and changeth not.
He that putteth not out his money to usury,
nor taketh reward against the innocent.
He that doeth these things shall never be moved.

PSALM 15

THE LORD IS MY SHEPHERD;
I shall not want.
He maketh me to lie down in green
pastures: he leadeth me beside the still waters.
He restoreth my soul: he leadeth me in
the paths of righteousness for his name's sake.
Yea, though I walk through the valley of
the shadow of death, I will fear no evil:
for thou art with me; thy rod and thy staff
they comfort me.

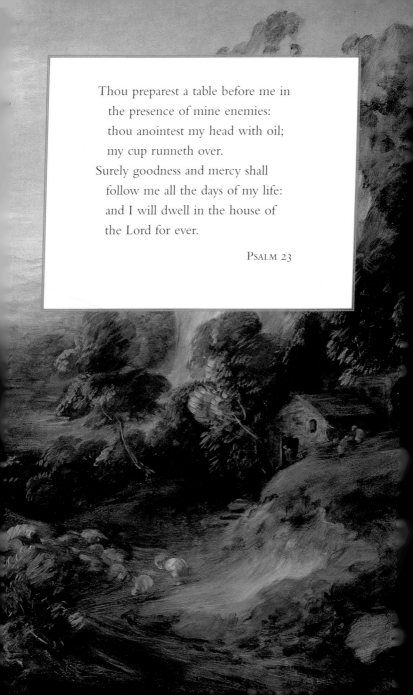

Thou preparest a table before me in
the presence of mine enemies:
thou anointest my head with oil;
my cup runneth over.
Surely goodness and mercy shall
follow me all the days of my life:
and I will dwell in the house of
the Lord for ever.

PSALM 23

T HE LORD is my light and my
salvation; whom shall I fear?
The Lord is the strength of
my life; of whom shall I be afraid?

from PSALM 27

ONE THING have I desired of the Lord, that will I seek after; that I may dwell in the house of the Lord all the days of my life, to behold the beauty of the Lord, and to enquire in his temple.

from PSALM 27

AS THE HART PANTETH
after the water brooks, so panteth
my soul after thee, O God.
My soul thirsteth for God, for the living God:
  when shall I come and appear before God?
My tears have been my meat day and night,
  while they continually say unto me,
  Where is thy God?
When I remember these things,
  I pour out my soul in me:
  for I had gone with the multitude,
  I went with them to the house of God,
  with the voice of joy and praise,
  with a multitude that kept holyday.
Why art thou cast down, O my soul?
  and why art thou disquieted in me?
  hope thou in God: for I shall yet praise him
  for the help of his countenance.

from PSALM 42

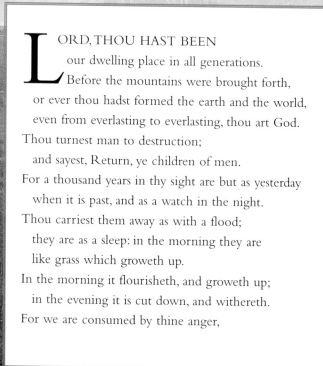

LORD, THOU HAST BEEN
our dwelling place in all generations.
Before the mountains were brought forth,
or ever thou hadst formed the earth and the world,
even from everlasting to everlasting, thou art God.
Thou turnest man to destruction;
and sayest, Return, ye children of men.
For a thousand years in thy sight are but as yesterday
when it is past, and as a watch in the night.
Thou carriest them away as with a flood;
they are as a sleep: in the morning they are
like grass which groweth up.
In the morning it flourisheth, and groweth up;
in the evening it is cut down, and withereth.
For we are consumed by thine anger,

and by thy wrath are we troubled.

Thou hast set our iniquities before thee,
   our secret sins in the light of thy countenance.

For all our days are passed away in thy wrath:
   we spend our years as a tale that is told.

The days of our years are threescore years
   and ten; and if by reason of strength they be
   fourscore years, yet is their strength labour and
   sorrow; for it is soon cut off, and we fly away.

Who knoweth the power of thine anger?
   even according to thy fear, so is thy wrath.

So teach us to number our days, that we may
   apply our hearts unto wisdom.

from PSALM 90

HE THAT DWELLETH in the secret place
of the most High shall abide under
the shadow of the Almighty.
I will say of the Lord, He is my refuge
and my fortress: my God; in him will I trust.
Surely he shall deliver thee from the snare
of the fowler, and from the noisome pestilence.
He shall cover thee with his feathers, and under
his wings shalt thou trust: his truth shall be
thy shield and buckler.
Thou shalt not be afraid for the terror by night;
nor for the arrow that flieth by day;
Nor for the pestilence that walketh in darkness;
nor for the destruction that wasteth at noonday.
A thousand shall fall at thy side, and ten thousand
at thy right hand; but it shall not come nigh thee.
Only with thine eyes shalt thou behold and see
the reward of the wicked.
Because thou hast made the Lord, which is my refuge,
even the most High, thy habitation;
There shall no evil befall thee, neither shall
any plague come nigh thy dwelling.
For he shall give his angels charge over thee,
to keep thee in all thy ways.

from PSALM 91

EXCEPT THE LORD build the house,
they labour in vain that build it:
except the Lord keep the city,
the watchman waketh but in vain.
It is vain for you to rise up early, to sit up late,
to eat the bread of sorrows: for so he giveth
his beloved sleep.
Lo, children are an heritage of the Lord:
and the fruit of the womb is his reward.
As arrows are in the hand of a mighty man;
so are children of the youth.
Happy is the man that hath his quiver full
of them: they shall not be ashamed,
but they shall speak with the enemies
in the gate.

PSALM 127

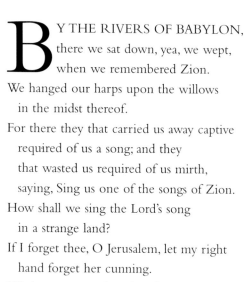

BY THE RIVERS OF BABYLON,
there we sat down, yea, we wept,
when we remembered Zion.
We hanged our harps upon the willows
in the midst thereof.
For there they that carried us away captive
required of us a song; and they
that wasted us required of us mirth,
saying, Sing us one of the songs of Zion.
How shall we sing the Lord's song
in a strange land?
If I forget thee, O Jerusalem, let my right
hand forget her cunning.
If I do not remember thee, let my tongue
cleave to the roof of my mouth; if I prefer
not Jerusalem above my chief joy.

from PSALM 137

O LORD, thou hast searched me,
and known me.
Thou knowest my downsitting
and mine uprising, thou understandest
my thought afar off.
Thou compassest my path and my lying down,
and art acquainted with all my ways.
For there is not a word in my tongue,
but, lo, O Lord, thou knowest it altogether.
Thou hast beset me behind and before,
and laid thine hand upon me.
Such knowledge is too wonderful for me;
it is high, I cannot attain unto it.
Whither shall I go from thy spirit?
Or whither shall I flee from thy presence?
If I ascend up into heaven, thou art there:
if I make my bed in hell, behold, thou art there.
If I take the wings of the morning,
and dwell in the uttermost parts of the sea;
Even there shall thy hand lead me,
and thy right hand shall hold me.

from PSALM 139

I WILL LIFT UP mine eyes unto
the hills, from whence cometh my help.
My help cometh from the Lord,
which made heaven and earth.
He will not suffer thy foot to be moved:
he that keepeth thee will not slumber.
Behold, he that keepeth Israel
shall neither slumber nor sleep.
The Lord is thy keeper: the Lord is thy shade
upon thy right hand.
The sun shall not smite thee by day,
nor the moon by night.
The Lord shall preserve thee from all evil:
he shall preserve thy soul.
The Lord shall preserve thy going out and
thy coming in from this time forth,
and even for evermore.

PSALM 121

INDEX OF ARTISTS AND PAINTINGS

PAGES 10–11

Heaven *from* The Last Judgement

GIOVANNI DE PAOLO
(active by 1417; died 1482)

Pinacoteca Nazionale, Siena

PAGES 14–15

The Last Judgement (*detail*)

GIOTTO DI BONDONE
(*c.* 1266–1337)

Cappella degli Scrovegni, Padua

PAGE 12

Saint Cecilia

CARLO SARACENI
(1579–1620)

Galleria Nazionale d'Arte Antica, Rome

PAGE 18

Assumption of Mary (*detail*)

PIETRO PERUGINO
(living 1469; died 1523)

Galleria dell'Accademia, Florence

PAGES 16–17

German Mountain Landscape (*detail*)

CASPAR DAVID FRIEDRICH
(1774–1840)

Gemäldegalerie, Dresden

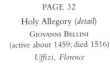

PAGE 41

Enthroned Virgin Mary
with Child (*detail*)
ANTONIO DA NEGROPONTE
(active *c.* 1470)
*Cappella Morosini, San Francesco della
Vigna, Venice*

PAGE 42

Saint Jerome in a Rocky
Landscape (*detail*)
Attributed to JOACHIM PATENIER
(active 1515; died not later
than 1524)
The National Gallery, London

PAGES 44–45

The Agony in the Garden (*detail*)
GIOVANNI BELLINI
(active about 1459; died 1516)
The National Gallery, London

PAGE 46

Tobias and the Angel (*detail*)
TITIAN
(active about 1506; died 1576)
Galleria dell'Accademia, Venice

PAGE 48

The Last Supper (*detail*)
ANDREA DEL CASTAGNO
(*c.* 1421–1457)
Santa Apollonia, Florence

PAGES 50–51

English Landscape with Bridge (*detail*)
THOMAS GAINSBOROUGH
(1727–1788)
National Gallery of Art, Washington

PAGES 52 and 53

The Virgin of the
Rocks (*details*)
LEONARDO DA VINCI
(1452–1519)
Louvre, Paris

PAGE 55

The Wilton Diptych
(*reverse panel*)
UNKNOWN ENGLISH OR
FRENCH ARTIST
(active *c.* 1395)
*The National Gallery,
London*

PAGE 56–57

Joshua Commanding the Sun
to Stand Still (*detail*)
JOHN MARTIN
(1789–1854)
Private Collection

PAGE 59
The Angel with the Lily
GUARIENTO
(active 1338; died *c.* 1368/70)
Museo Civici, Padua

PAGE 60
Mary Worshipping the Sleeping Child (*detail*)
ALVISE VIVARINI
(living 1457; died 1503/5)
Il Redentore, Venice

PAGES 62–63
Landscape with Mourning Jews (*detail*)
FERDINAND OLIVIER
(1785–1841)
Behnhaus, Lübeck

PAGE 65
Jeremiah Lamenting the
Destruction of Jerusalem
REMBRANDT
(1606–1669)
Rijksmuseum, Amsterdam

PAGES 66–67
The Stigmatization of St Francis
of Assisi at La Verna (*detail*)
DOMENICO GHIRLANDAIO
(1449–1494)
Cappella Sassetti, San Tranita, Florence

Index of First Lines

Photographic Acknowledgments

For permission to reproduce the paintings on the
following pages and for supplying photographs,
the Publishers would like to thank:

AKG London:18, 32, 34 and 35, 41, 42, 62–63, 65;

AKG/Cameraphoto 5, 14–15, 23, 38, 46,

59, 60, endpapers; AKG/S. Domingie 66–67;

AKG/Erich Lessing 20–21, 55

The Art Archive: 16–17, 28–29, 30–31,

44–45, 48, 50–51, 52 and 53, 56–57

The J. Paul Getty Museum: 6, 36

Scala, Florence: 8, 10–11,12, 25, 26–27